THE JOURNEY OF
BROKENNESS

THE JOURNEY OF
BROKENNESS

HERB BRISBANE

XULON PRESS

Xulon Press
2301 Lucien Way #415
Maitland, FL 32751
407.339.4217
www.xulonpress.com

Printed in the United States of America.

ISBN-13: 9781545617090

FOREWORD:

In his book, *The Root of the Righteous*, Aiden Wilson Tozer wrote, "It is doubtful whether God can bless man a *greatly* (italics mine) until he has hurt [broken] him *deeply*" (italics mine). In *The Journey of Brokenness*, Reverend Herb Brisbane, a journeyman, an experienced preacher, shares his journey of being deeply broken and greatly blessed. The reader is invited to eavesdrop on his soliloquy (his conversation with himself) and his colloquy (his conversation with God) to view his odyssey through a window that at times narrows to a slit and to walk alongside him on a path that is thin, slippery, and extremely narrow.

One of the areas in which preaching, teaching, and witnessing is deficient is that of personal *witness*. There is much personal *address* in proclaiming truth to others from the outside, but not enough personal *witness* of sharing truth from within. In this work the author in "the already" of time joins the ranks of those in "the not yet" of eternity who are credited with "overcoming by the blood and their testimony" (Revelation 12:11).

This is not a secondhand account—it is Herb Brisbane's story. Like a phoenix, the author rises from the ashes of personal and family crises and physical illness, which threatened to terminate his life to sing, "This is my story, this is my song. Praising my Savior all the day long."

In his autobiographical sketch, the author acknowledges his journey is not complete; yet he trusts in a God who "has begun a good work and will complete it in the day of Christ Jesus" (Philippians 1:6). Caution: If you are allergic to reality and authenticity; if you want a Christianity that is palatable without being spiritually profitable; if you are only willing to receive the blessings of life without the burdens; and if you only want God to be a theological bell hop and ecclesiastical red cap without being the sovereign Lord who orders both our *steps* and our *stops*, then this book is **not** for you. But, if you are willing to trust a God who allowed His only Son to be *broken* while taking bread and *breaking* it and giving it to the disciples and saying, "This is my body broken for you" (Luke 22:19), and then rise from the grave with resurrection power, then this book is not just a book for you to read; it is a book you **must** read! You will discover in reading this account there is joy *in* the journey not simply at the *end* of the journey.

Dr. Robert Smith, Jr.
Charles T. Carter Baptist Chair of Divinity
Beeson Divinity School
Samford University

TABLE OF CONTENTS

PROLOGUE

It happened on a routine Monday afternoon. I am a voluntary chaplain at Grapevine Baylor Scott and White Hospital. It was a beautiful day, but I didn't feel like going in to work. Something on the inside of me kept saying I needed to show up. The Lord impressed upon my heart if I just showed up, He would stand up in me. I went to the chaplain office to receive my list for the day of whom I was to visit. The list included the name of the patient, age, room number, and religion. I prayed, as I would always do, to encourage, inspire, and be a good listener and a witness for the Lord.

As I started walking down the hall, I noticed my first patient was of Jewish decent. It has been my experience that this group of people normally does not want a visit from the chaplain. I almost passed this room up, but the Lord impressed upon my heart to knock on the door. She was in her mid-forties and as I entered her room, she gave me a look as if to say, "Why are you here?" She was slightly reserved and I could tell she wanted me to leave and go to the next room, but the Lord spoke to my heart saying, "This is where I want you to be." The Lord said, "I just want you to listen to her and let her tell her story."

So for the next forty-five minutes, I listened to her as she shared about her life. She was a world traveler, but she talked about an experience that happened to her in Palestine while she was in Jerusalem. She told me an incident changed her life and she started to spiral downward. She never got over that experience. She said it had led her down to a dark path.

Then she said to me, "You wouldn't know anything about darkness."

It was at that moment that God said, "Now it's time for you to talk and share your testimony."

I told her that I had an experience of something that had happened to me about three years prior. I told her that cancer had invaded my body and I almost died, but it was the Lord who rescued me from this deadly illness. I shared with her that I had been in depression for three years. My life was surrounded by darkness, but it was my faith in Jesus Christ that kept me.

She began to weep and it occurred to me why I had to come to work that day. I told her that over 2,000 years ago, Jesus suffered bled and died on an old rugged cross for the sins of mankind. I shared with her that he stayed in the grave for three days but early that day which was on a Sunday that God raised Him up from the grave with all power in Heaven and Earth. He paid a price that He did not owe and we owed a price we could not pay. I shared with her Romans 10:9: "if you confess with your mouth the Lord Jesus and believe in your heart that God has raised Him from the dead, you will be saved."

I asked her if she wanted to accept Jesus as her personal savior. With tears in her eyes she said yes. I then led her in a short prayer. It was at that time the light shined through the blinds . She then asked me if she could take a picture of me, because she wanted to remember the person who led her to Jesus.

Well, I knew my task was finished. As I began to leave the room, I told her to find a good church and read the Bible daily. She was the only patient I saw that day and there were no interruptions of doctors or nurses during this time.

Chapter One:

LIFE BEGINS

T he nickname given to me by one of my teachers was "Preacher." I was in the fourth grade at the time. I had no idea that it would be prophetic.

That calling continued throughout my teen years. I remember one afternoon while resting in my bedroom, I heard a voice calling my name. I went into the living room where my grandmother, Mrs. Delia Tatum, was in her favorite chair.

I asked her, "Did you call me?"

She replied, "No, I didn't."

I went back to my bedroom, and after a while, I heard a voice calling my name. I immediately ran to Grandmother and asked if she had called me.

She answered, "No, I did not call you."

When I returned to my room, the voice called for the third time. Returning to my grandmother, I shared with her that I was baffled about the voice. She told me to call my stepfather who was a pastor.

I explained to him what had happened to me, and he told me to turn in my Bible to 1 Samuel 3: 1-10. These are the words that I read:

> And the child Samuel ministered unto the Lord before
> Eli. And the word of the Lord was precious in those
> days, there was no open vision. And it came to pass

at that time, when Eli was laid down in his place, and his eyes began to was dim, that he could not see; and ere the lamp of God went out in the temple of the Lord, where the ark of God was, and Samuel was laid down to sleep; that the Lord called Samuel: and he answered, "Here am I." And he ran into Eli, and said, "Here am I; for thou calledst me." And he said, "I called not; lie down again." And he went and lay down. And the Lord called yet again, "Samuel." And Samuel arose and went to Eli, and said, "Here am I; for thou didst call me." And he answered, "I called not, my son; lie down again." Now Samuel did not yet know the Lord, neither was the word of the Lord yet revealed unto him. And the Lord called Samuel again the third time. And he arose and went to Eli, and said, "Here am I; for thou didst call me." And Eli perceived that the Lord had called the child. Therefore Eli said unto Samuel, "Go, lie down: and it shall be, if He call thee, that thou shalt say, 'Speak, Lord; for thy servant heareth.'" So Samuel went and lay down in his place. And the Lord came, and stood, and called as at other times," Samuel, Samuel." Then Samuel answered, "Speak; for thy servant heareth."

I read these Scriptures and meditated over them.
I then said, "Speak, Lord."
There was no answer. Only silence. Since I was only thirteen years old, I kept this experience in the back of my mind and pondered what it meant for my life. I went to church every Sunday and grew in the Lord. I did not want to preach because I intended to be a professional baseball player. I thought I could fulfill this dream because I excelled in many sports: football, basketball, baseball, and track. Now I saw what God had planned all those years back. He knew what I was supposed to do in life, and that was not professional sports.

There was an event that happened my senior year in high school that changed the direction of my life. I was a star basketball player whose success on the court was chronicled in the newspaper weekly. I was happy with my life and the direction it was headed.

One night, I was getting ready to go out with some of my friends for the evening, but my curfew was midnight. They were late picking me up. My grandmother told me of a dream she had where there were three police cars and an ambulance involved. I jokingly told her it was probably something she had eaten before she went to sleep that gave her heartburn. Finally, my friends arrived, and we headed to pick up another friend. As we turned the corner approaching our friend's house, we saw people running and crying. We got to his yard and saw him lying on the ground. He had been shot. If we had been there on time, we could also have been shot.

As I sat in the hospital waiting for news about him, the Lord spoke to my heart and said that I could have been the one lying on the ground. He warned me to give up a bad habit that I had acquired. Then my grandmother's dream rushed to my mind because three police cars and one ambulance were at the scene.

I had a good senior year both as a student and as a basketball player. I made the All Tournament Team three times, and I was named Most Valuable Player. I have to give credit to my great high school coach, Bubba Bailey, who showed me how to have a strong inside game against taller opponents. I was listed as 6'3", but I was probably closer to 6'2 ½". His teaching prepared me for playing against 6'6" and 6'7" players in college. I was a forward and not a guard.

Chapter Two:

LESSONS I LEARNED FROM MY GRANDMOTHER

G rowing up, I watched my grandmother's relationship with her Lord. She began each morning by reading her Bible and praying. Her actions impressed on me the importance of spending time each day communing with the Lord. It was her faithfulness to the Lord that brought me to salvation through our Lord Jesus Christ. I wanted that peace and assurance she possessed as she grew closer daily to her Savior.

Not only was she a faithful Christian, but she also was a fantastic cook. Since I was a growing boy, I enjoyed this gift of hers daily. She made most of her meals from scratch. As she cooked her delicious food, she would hum her favorite hymns. Some of her most memorable meals consisted of chicken and dumplings, steak, and pork chops, followed by cakes covered with chocolate or lemon icing.

Another lesson she taught me was to love the people around me. She had a great relationship with our community. People came to our house almost every day wanting to borrow eggs, sugar, milk, or some other food supplies. I remember an incident when a homeless man showed up at our door asking for food. That morning, Grandma had cooked several pork chops. I had eaten two, but I put back two more for my lunch. Grandma invited the stranger in and told him she would fix him something to eat. She began to look for the extra pork chops. Knowing her intent, I had hidden them so I could have them later. As she searched the kitchen, she soon found my hiding place. She fed the man my two pork chops. Noticing my sad look, she realized I had wanted them for myself. She used this time to explain to me that God wanted us to fed the hungry and care for those less fortunate than we were. We did not have much, but she willingly gave out of her meager resources. As a child, I observed just as God had supplied the needs of Elijah in 1 Kings 17:9-16, He would supply our daily needs also.

She encouraged me to always look my best because I was the child of King Jesus. I remember the Easter Sunday that she presented me with a new suit when I was about ten years old. It was a beautiful green suit that changed colors in the sunlight. When I left for church, she reminded me not to play in my new suit so that I would not get it dirty or torn. Putting those words completely out of my mind the minute I left the house, several friends and I decided to play a game that required running. Of course, I fell and tore the pants of my new suit.

I devised a plan to keep Grandma from finding out that I had disobeyed her. She always sat in her favorite chair, which faced the front door. I chose to come in the back door so that she would not see my torn pants.

After a couple of months, she asked me why I had not been wearing my new suit. I informed her that I really didn't like it. She told me to get the suit and bring it to her. I slowly brought it with the pants that I had tried to repair. My sewing skills were not good, so my stitches didn't hold. I then tried to glue the knee together with bubble gum, but that didn't work. Even though she was angry with me for the deception, she had to laugh as she saw the poor attempts that I had made to repair the pants.

She told my aunt to take me to S&Q Clothiers and buy me a new suit. Over the years, she would think of that incident and laugh. I learned we all make mistakes, but our shortcomings are forgiven by those who love us just as our Lord forgives us when we sin and ask for forgiveness.

Grandma and I enjoyed many things together. We both loved the soap opera, "The Young and the Restless." We watched it every day. Her ordinary routine was to go to bed early, but since I wanted to learn to play dominos, she stayed up one night until midnight, showing me how to play. I finally got the hang of it, and I now can hold my own against most people. She loved me in my own language when I was young. Her loving me that way taught me how to love other people in their own language.

Grandma taught me as a teenager to manage money. She encouraged me to develop a line of credit. I had cards from S&Q Clothiers and Levine's. She monitored my credit and kept me in check until I became an adult. Each month she tucked away a little money, folded in paper, in her apron pocket. As an adult, I remember times after I left home that she would pull twenty-five dollars from that pocket and give it to me. She was a good steward of the money God gave her.

Not only did she have the gift of giving, but she also was blessed with wisdom. Grandma was an encourager, just like Silas. She spoke ill of no one. She talked with countless people and listened attentively to their problems. She never put other people's business in the streets. Her advice was based on the Word of God. Many of these people's concerns were discovered through her incredible phone ministry. She never wrote numbers in a book because she was capable of storing all of them in her sharp mind. If she had not heard recently from her friends, she would call to check on them. Friendship meant a great deal to her.

My mother's twin sister and her two sons lived with us. Aunt Margaret contributed to the household expenses by working for a Jewish family for many years. Grandma's son, who was in the military, sent her a monthly stipend. By pooling the money, she always managed to pay her account at the local grocery store in full each month and to save enough money for us to purchase a home.

We lived in the projects from my kindergarten years until my junior year in high school when the Lord allowed us to buy our home. Grandma's giving, wisdom, and excellent money management endeared us to our community. She had made such a difference in many lives there that when we left, many people showed up to bid us a tearful goodbye. We also experienced some sadness as we left our well-manicured yard, those beautiful rose bushes, and Grandma's garden in the backyard as we moved to our new home.

Many of her strong values were ingrained in me. I recognize many times her influence on my life as I grow older. My relationship with my grandmother shaped the man that I later became.

Chapter Three:

INTO THE DEEP

At the end of my high school career, I wanted to attend college, but my grandmother could not afford to send me. She told me to work on my skills as hard as I could, and she would pray as hard as she could. I was offered a few scholarships to junior colleges, but I wanted to be closer to home.

That summer, the coach from Midwestern University, located in my hometown, visited me at my mother's home. He offered me a one-year scholarship. In our meeting, he made a comment that I considered unusual. He said I was a suspect. He explained I had a good senior year, but he didn't know if I could play college ball. My mother, who was a kind, smart, faithful servant of the Lord, was happy about my receiving the scholarship. I immediately rushed home to share the good news with Grandmother, who was thrilled. When I told her about the coach's remark about being a suspect and not a prospect, she advised me to put in the time training for the season, and she would continue to pray for me. I played every day at the YMCA.

I entered college that fall and found myself playing against talented players from California, New York, Florida, Kentucky, Indiana, and several other states. It was a major transition from high school basketball to college ball. The first half of my freshman year season, I didn't get to play much. I was a little disappointed and thought about transferring to another school. When I told my grandmother, she wisely counseled me that I could not run away from challenges just because things got a little tough. Her voice has spoken to my spirit many times as I faced similar challenges.

The middle of December of my freshman year, two of our starters did not make their grades and had to leave school. I went from not playing at all to being on the starting five. The Lord blessed me with a good second half of the season by rewarding me with a three-year scholarship. Our team went to the National Championship my junior year. As a result of my performing my famous "back door" move, I was listed in *Sports Illustrated* magazine. My time there brings Galatians 6:9 to mind: "And let us not be weary in well doing, for in due season, we shall reap if we faint not."

When I was nineteen, I finished my second year of college where I played basketball on scholarship. Everything was going well. However, one day after class I started crying. Since I was a good student, I had not failed any tests. I had no idea why I was upset enough to cry. I had skipped basketball practice, so a good friend of mine, who was an all American player, came looking for me. When he found me under a tree crying, he asked me what was wrong. I explained I had realized I had been running from my call to ministry. I got up and rushed to call my grandmother, a woman of great wisdom, to share with her the feelings I had.

Following her suggestion, I went to visit my pastor. He wasn't surprised about my call. After counseling with me, he instructed me to go forward on Sunday during the invitation and proclaim publicly my call to the ministry. That public commitment to God's plan for my life filled me with a sense of peace. My mind was pulled back to my vision at the age of thirteen, and now I saw what God had planned all those years back. He knew what I was going to be led to do, but I had not put it together. Now my purpose was clear.

The second milestone began when I was a freshman at Midwestern. A beautiful cheerleader, Sheila Martin, caught my eye. Since she cheered for our team, we became good friends.

Summer came, and school was out. I experienced an empty feeling in my heart when she went home. I was looking forward to the beginning of school because I would be able to see Sheila. When we met again, we shared how we had missed each other. One evening, while walking around the campus, I asked her to marry me. She surprised me by accepting my proposal. We got married her senior year. I was two years behind her, so I continued with school. We lived on her teaching salary and the married stipend I received from the college. We decided to delay starting a family until I graduated. With her support and encouragement, I graduated two years later.

I began my new job at the bank, and two months later, we found out she was expecting. Thrilled with the news, we began to buy baby clothes. In the back of my mind, I knew it was too early to be stocking the nursery because we had seven more months to go. Our excitement continued until the fifth month of her pregnancy. She was diagnosed with toxemia, an abnormal condition where toxic substances are located in the blood. This illness made her feet and ankles swell, and she was very sick. She worked until the doctor ordered complete bed rest. Our income dropped significantly since she was unable to work. I was torn because I wanted to stay with her, but now I had to go to work to support us. I called my pastor, Reverend R.M. Castle, and explained our critical situation. He shared with one of the mission groups in our church our dilemma. They took turns staying with my wife and cooking for her. I will always be eternally grateful to my pastor and those ladies for their care during this difficult time.

In the seventh month of her pregnancy, the doctor hospitalized her. One Sunday morning after I had finished preaching, I made my way to the hospital to spend some time with her. Unaware of the subtle change in her condition, I fulfilled her request to read the twenty-third Psalm to her. Afterward, we visited for a while, and she then encouraged me to go home to rest. Even though I protested, she insisted. She said she was tired and ready to go to sleep. I went home intending to rest, but all I could do was toss and turn.

I had an uneasy feeling that something was wrong. I eventually drifted off to sleep, only to be awakened by the phone at two in the morning. The doctor informed me that we had lost our son, and he was not sure if my wife would survive. I rushed to the hospital to see her, but she had fallen into a coma.

For three days every hour on the hour, I uttered three words: "I love you." I prayed fervently that God would bring her out of the coma. He answered my prayer on the third day. So excited, I grabbed her hand and assured her that everything was going to be all right. With tears in her eyes, she took my hand and shook her head. She fell in the coma again. With tears in my eyes and a heavy heart, I made my way to the chapel to pray. About twenty minutes later, the doctor found me and informed me that my wife had passed away.

My whole world was blown apart. I didn't know how I would survive without her. I cried until no tears were left; my heart was torn in pieces. The pain was so deep that I felt as if I were on the brink of death myself. I embraced her mother, and we sobbed together. My stepfather, Reverend Floyd Chenault, and my mother, Marjorie Chenault, brothers and sister offered encouraging words after they received the news of Sheila's death. I finally went to tell my grandmother about Sheila.

The first question I asked her was, "Why did God let my wife and son die?"

After pausing to search for an answer, she replied, "I don't know, but trust in the Lord."

We had funerals for Sheila and our son on the same day. One was in the morning in Wichita Falls, Texas, and the other was in Dallas, Texas, that afternoon. The church was packed that morning with both black and white friends. The people of Wichita Falls had been praying for us because we were well known and loved there. We then turned our cars south toward Dallas for the two-and-a-half-hour drive to her home church. That service was well attended, too.

In the next few months, I felt hurt and lost. My best friend and our son were no longer a part of my life. My life felt like it lost its meaning. I was only twenty-one years old and on the hopeless brink of an emotional death.

Three months later, I was hit with another tragedy. My father died of cancer. Since he and my mother had divorced when I was a baby, I had not had any contact with him; however, we had connected a year before his death. He was in the military and traveled a great deal. He knew that I lived with my grandmother because he financially supported me, but we had not met face to face. He had been aware of my activities because my sister in Washington, D.C. had corresponded with me and collected newspaper articles about my sports involvement. She shared this information with my brothers and my father's family.

When I met my father, I was shocked at how much we looked alike and shared the same mannerisms. I was just getting to know him when he passed away. Even though my grandmother had raised me to love my father, I had difficulty with trusting men because my father figure had always been absent from my life. However, my uncle, Reverend J.C. White, served as a father figure by coaching me in Little League baseball. He mentored me, helping me to choose the right road.

The pain from the recent loss of my wife and son kept me from attending my father's funeral. I didn't think I could bear any more grief. I felt as if I were in a deep hole surrounded by darkness with almost no hope.

Chapter Four:

OUT OF THE DEEP

S everal months after Sheila and my son's passing, I received a phone call that challenged my heart. Dr. Bill Pinson, pastor of First Baptist Church in Wichita Falls, asked me to come to his office to talk and pray. He shared that he had kept up with me throughout my college basketball career.

He asked, "What are you going to do now?"

I informed him that I was currently working at a bank and hoped to move up the ladder in that institution. He told me about a scholarship that was available to Southwestern Baptist Theological Seminary in Ft. Worth for a person who wanted to go into full time ministry. I thanked him and told him I would think about it. As soon as I left his office, I completely dismissed the idea.

Just as I opened the door to my apartment, the phone rang. It was my mother-in-law checking on me. Her words blew my mind.

She said, "Don't let my daughter's death go to waste. God has something great in store for you."

Thinking about my conversation with her, my mind was drawn back to the meeting that I had just left. Grandmother had taught me to always pray before making any major decision. I felt compelled to pray, pray, and pray some more. A peace fell over me, and I knew God had given me direction. I resigned from my job and left home to attend seminary in the fall.

My boss at the bank tried to talk me out of resigning because they had big plans for me. The chairman of the bank was also one of the trustees at Midwestern University where I had attended college. He had groomed me for four years by introducing me to certain people and mentoring me in the banking business. My job was certain and offered the security that I wanted, but God began to talk to my heart. As I wrestled with the decision, I was led back to the peace that God had given me when I decided to resign. I knew what my choice had to be.

To affirm my decision, I believe God gave me another sign. The evening before I left for Ft. Worth, a big storm blew in. As I gazed out the window, I noticed a tree being bent almost to the ground by the high wind. Then a strange thing happened. The storm eased, and a rainbow appeared in the sky. I felt the Lord speak to my heart.

He said, "Your life has been like that tree. There have been storms that have tossed you from side to side, but like that tree, you are not going to break. I will put a rainbow in your life after the storms have passed."

The next day, I started my new journey as I headed toward Ft. Worth. I was committed because I believed this was God's will. When I arrived at the seminary, I found that housing was full, so I was placed on a waiting list. I rented a room at a hotel. Since it cost me four hundred dollars for a month, I knew I could not live there for four years.

One week later, I found an apartment that rented for two hundred dollars a month. I returned to the hotel to ask for a refund for the three weeks that I would not be living there. They were reluctant to return my money, but God intervened. I stayed in the furnished apartment for about a month. Something prodded me to go by the seminary and check on student housing. They informed me that they had been trying to reach me because housing was now available. I was able to move in immediately. Rent was only sixty dollars a month. God had once again taken care of me. Whatever God orders, He pays for.

I had been in school for three months, and I began to wonder if I had made the right decision. I was taking some difficult classes, especially baby Greek. I soon found out why it had acquired that name. It kept me up all night and made me want to cry. All of these problems made me doubt the choice I had made.

I had visited several churches, but I didn't feel that any one of those was the place I needed to serve. I finally went to the church recommended by my pastor. Shiloh Missionary Baptist was the church, and the pastor was the late Reverend A.E. Chew. I really enjoyed the service, but I still missed my home church. The next Saturday evening arrived, but I didn't feel like going to church the next day. However, God impressed upon my heart that I needed to attend. As I sat in the pulpit area with several of my young minister friends, I suddenly saw a tall, slender, beautiful young lady walk in. She looked like a model. I asked the minister next to me if he knew who she was. He informed me that she was his cousin.

I replied, "Praise the Lord!"

I could hardly wait until the end of the service so that he could introduce me to her. I fell head over heels in love with her the minute we met. We talked for a bit, and I asked her for a date for that night. She accepted. When I picked her up, I had put in a tape. I wasn't sure if she thought it was going to be "Nearer My God to Thee" or some other hymn, but I had chosen Barry White singing, "Close to You." Her strange look made me feel that she might be afraid she had made a mistake in accepting the date. We had a wonderful conversation at our meal, and I finally shared with her the story of my losing my wife and child almost a year before. Her reply was unforgettable.

"The Lord is going to catch all your tears and put them in a divine vase. After it is filled up, He will tilt over the vase, and the tears are going to turn into blessings."

I had never heard any words of comfort like that before, and I could feel hope coming back into my heart. I felt real joy return to me as I thought about her that night. I thanked the Lord for leading me to church that Sunday.

Wanda and I became inseparable after that evening. After dating for a while, I was reminded by the Lord of the double rainbow that He had shown me when I was leaving home to come to seminary. I then knew she was the one God had chosen for me. After a short period of time, I went to her parents' home where she lived. I assume she thought I was there to ask her for another date because she seemed surprised when I asked her to marry me. She accepted my proposal. She told me that she and her parents had been praying for approximately a year that the Lord would send her the man He wanted her to marry. She felt I was the one He had chosen.

Her parents were happy that God had answered their prayers. I then took her home to meet my grandmother. The two ladies immediately liked each other. Grandmother, with her great wisdom, knew Wanda was a kind person and would be a good wife for me. Just as He had done for Job, God restored me with my wife and best friend. Our love story has been and continues going on after forty years of marriage.

The book of Job has a new and deeper meaning to me as I see how our lives have had numerous parallels. Chapters 1 and 2 deal with Job's losses, but Chapter 42 shows how God restored fourteen thousand sheep, six thousand camels, a thousand yoke of oxen, and a thousand donkeys to him. He gave him seven sons and three daughters after his other children were taken from him.

The Lord restored me with the birth of three children. Marlin, who attended Prairie View University, and Melissa, are the parents of three of our grandchildren: Marleigh, Mason, and Maxwell. He is an entrepreneur who has his own hydration business. Tennille graduated from Baylor University with a bachelor's degree, and then she earned her master's degree in Commerce from Texas A&M. She is presently working as a licensed social worker in the Children's Hospital in Dallas. She is married to Cedric, and they have C.J., their three-year-old son. Marcus, a graduate of Liberty University, works for the Government. His wife is Ruth. Our God is so good.

Chapter Five:

THE LONG JOURNEY

I graduated with my Master's Degree in Divinity in December 1980 and was offered a job at Sam Houston State University as Associate Baptist Student Union Director. On January 1981, my ministry began under the covering of the Southern Baptist Convention. I am appreciative to the Southern Baptists, who gave me a scholarship for my three-year stay in graduate school and for my first two jobs.

I did not know about student work until my final year in seminary. I was taking a heavy course load with Greek, Hebrew, New Testament, and Systematic Theology. I was looking for an easy crib course. I decided it was a Baptist Student Director class. Dr. Howard, the professor who had been B.S.U. State Director for many years, took an interest in me. The Lord gave me favor with him, and he gave me my first part time job as B.S.U. Director for Tarrant County Junior College, South Campus. This was a great learning experience. I had a core group that was diverse. This positive experience opened the door for my going to Sam Houston State University, a predominately Anglo University in Huntsville, Texas.

It was such a blessing because my first supervisor was the B.S.U. director at Midwestern University from where I had gotten my bachelor's degree. His name was Don Coleman. At Midwestern, he had given me a surprise banquet at the B.S.U. student union building to celebrate our playing in the National Championship in Kansas. I was presented a trophy that seemed as tall as I was.

At Sam Houston, my responsibilities were to encourage all students with an emphasis on reaching African American and International students. My goal was to help them grow in Christ and to understand and value each individual's culture. One of our greatest achievements was taking nearly two hundred students to the B.S.U. Convention at Baylor University. That experience began breaking down barriers. Half of the students were white and the other half was black. We all slept on the gym floor, and that experience opened the eyes of each group.

When my family and I arrived at Sam Houston State, each group looked us at suspiciously. The students began to accept me when our school played St. Mary's University. Robert Reid, a graduate of St. Mary's University and a player for the Houston Rockets, attended the game. We had played against each other in the semifinal game of the N.A.I.A. tournament which we won. This victory threw us into the National Championship game. I mentioned to the students that Robert and I had become acquainted with each other when we competed against each other in that game. I went over during halftime and talked with him. I brought him over to our group and introduced him. They were impressed, and I now had that credibility I had been lacking.

My second responsibility was to the international students. Since they were a long way from home, they often were lonely. We matched the B.S.U. students with them and helped them to read and speak English better by using the Bible as the principal tool. We also had a fellowship for them once a month. Sometimes our family would host this event in our small condo. The students didn't mind squeezing into a tight environment.

One morning, the Lord woke me early to walk around the campus. I knew it was the Lord because I am not an early riser. When I arrived on campus around 7:00, I noticed one of our international students crying. I took her to breakfast and listened to her story. She said she felt worthless because in her culture, a "C" grade was not valued or accepted. Since she had made a C in one of her classes, she considered dropping out of school. She was on the brink of giving up.

I shared with her my testimony of how I had lost my wife and son just a few years earlier. I explained my heart had been so broken that I wanted to give up, too. I shared that I could not have made it if it had not been for my faith in Jesus Christ. There were tears in her eyes as she listened. It occurred to me that the Lord woke me up early so that I could share Christ with her.

I asked her a question that gripped her heart. I asked her if she wanted to accept Jesus as her personal Savior. I explained He would love and embrace her just as she was. To my surprise, she said, "Yes." This was the first person from another country that I lead to the Lord. We both left with rejoicing in our heart. She became more involved in our B.S.U. through discipleship.

We stayed at Sam Houston for two-and-a-half years before the Lord opened the door for me to become the B.S.U. Director at Texas Southern University in Houston, Texas. This was a predominately African American university. In some respects, it was a culture shock to me. I tried to meet some students, but they looked at me suspiciously. I went home that day and shared my experience with my wife. She listened intently and told me that I needed to buy some different clothes so that they could relate to me. We went shopping, and sure enough, it began to open the door for conversation. These students were sharp and dressed as if they came out of *Ebony* magazine, which features successful black people who have made it to the top. I needed to reflect my success in the way I dressed.

Reaching these students at first was difficult because many of them had come to college hoping to spread their own wings and get out from under the watchful eye of their parents. Having church on campus was not their priority. I had to be innovative and use what I had. God pointed me to the gospel choir as a way to achieve acceptance. I developed a Bible study, which began about thirty minutes before their rehearsal. Over time, the study increased to an hour. My counseling ministry took off because of the pain and hurt that some of these students experienced in their relationships. Some guys had a sweet conversation and the looks to go with it. The relationship was fine for a while, but then hearts were broken.

I taught a Bible study that I called, "The grass may appear to be greener on the other side, but it might be AstroTurf." The ministry began to grow. I directed the attention of the students to missions. I emphasized they had been blessed to go to college, and they needed to help those who were less fortunate. My mind was drawn back to my childhood in the projects. I visited with parents in the local projects and asked if I could bring some college students to their recreation room to tutor their kids every week. The parents agreed, and all of us could see a change in the children's attitude. This project also changed the hearts of the college students who saw how important it was to be on mission for the Lord.

Our gospel choir sang at local churches to raise money to attend the National Black B.S.U. Retreat. Dr. John Corbitt was the national director. There were talented choirs from all over the country. One year, our choir placed in the top three in our category. We all were so happy, and I was named National Advisor for that year.

There were times I wondered if I had made any difference in this world. The Lord sent me an encourager just when I needed it. Twenty-five years after my time at Texas Southern University, I was on staff at a prestigious church. I was discouraged about my ministry. I got an email that day from a student that was at Texas Southern when I was there. He told me that I had made a difference in his life. He shared that he had not been involved with too many male mentors. He said I probably would not remember him, but he watched me from a distance to see if I lived what I preached. He finally came to trust me and shared his story with me. It was at a time when he chose which way his life would go. He was on the brink of his life. He needed to make some major decisions. I had forgotten about that conversation, but he told me he was now in the ministry because of the decisions he had made that day with my guidance.

The Lord reminded me of Psalm 1:1-3, which says:

> Blessed is the man that walked not in the counsel of the ungodly, nor standeth in the way of sinners, nor sitteth in the seat of the scornful. But his delight is in the law of the Lord; and in his law doth he meditate day and night. And he shall be like a tree planted by the rivers of water, that bringeth forth his fruit in his season; his leaf also shall not wither; and whatsoever he doeth shall prosper.

I was at Texas Southern for about two-and-a-half years. The Lord had allowed me to travel all over the state of Texas developing harambee groups on predominately Anglo American colleges. These groups were aimed at involving African American college students in Bible study and fellowship. I helped to form these Bible studies on many of the Texas college campuses.

The Lord put it into my heart to plan a statewide African American Retreat. This event was highly successful as we saw over three hundred students gather in Dallas, Texas, for a wonderful weekend. I asked my pastor, to be the speaker. I think he was surprised at the attendance. He did a wonderful job speaking to the students. He asked me before I introduced him if I had considered a Singles Ministry. We met the next week, and he shared his vision for singles. He offered me a staff position as Minister to Singles and Church Starting. My wife and I prayed over that offer and decided that the Lord led us to this position.

It was a mega church with eight thousand members; four thousand of those were singles. My pastor has one of the best church minds in the country. He mentored me on how to grow a church effectively. I watched him closely on how he led the church and its core leadership. I observed his leadership style and adopted some of it as my own. He shared with me the difference in pastoring a small church and a large one. According to Lyle Schaeller who was a National Church strategist said that the small church is like a farmer who does all the work. In a large church, the pastor is like a rancher who doesn't do all the work, but he makes sure it gets done. The pastor designates the right job to the right people. He explained that timing is critical to the life of a church. No major project should start unless the core leadership of the church agrees. He was able to remember the names of a majority of his congregation, and he was a servant leader, never asking his people to do things that he would not do himself. He gave me directions for the ministries that I was responsible for, but he allowed me to stretch them to another level.

My core singles group was comprised of lawyers, doctors, executives, and other professionals. I took some of them to a singles conference from another culture. We saw that it was good, but we needed to adapt it to meet our unique needs.

The next year, we started our own National Black Christian Singles Conference. Our pastor provided both advice and financial support for the conference. Our singles group became excited as they saw the project that they were a part of developing. My president of the National Conference, displayed great administrative gifts. She did a tremendous job in getting people involved. She encouraged me as the founder of this National Black Christian Singles Conference, which was hosted by our church.

God had given me a word for our local singles ministry: "I did not come here to help you get married." They were quite surprised, but I shared with them that I would help them be the best single they could be for the Lord. My emphasis was on Bible study and missions. I asked them to bring their special friends to the study so that they could grow in the Word together. Group dating was encouraged with activities that included attending plays or professional sports events.

The following year, we had several couples from our ministry to get married, and the ministry continued to grow. We chose relevant Bible studies. My favorite one was, "How to survive the loss of a love that is still walking around." We promoted it in the Sunday morning worship service. Singles came from all over the city, even from other churches. Many of these singles were on the brink of discouragement because of broken relationships. This study gave them a new lease on life.

My most favorite memory is one of our monthly mission projects, which met this time at a YMCA, located in a poor community and had not been cleaned out in years. We noticed the people in that neighborhood were suspiciously watching us. It seemed that all the cars that we came in were nice, new vehicles such as BMWs, Mercedes, Jaguars, and my older Chevrolet. The neighbors had no idea why we were there. When they saw we cleaned out the YMCA building, they joined in and helped us. I later discovered that one of the ladies who diligently cleaned was a corporate executive. The people who lived in that neighborhood realized we came to make life better for them and not to harm them.

Chapter Six:

JOY IN THE JOURNEY

O ne evening while watching television with my wife Wanda, and I said in a quiet voice, "Once this show goes off, I want you to take me to the hospital."

She replied, "What's wrong?"

I shared with her that I felt as if someone were standing on my chest. She quickly turned off the television and drove me frantically to the hospital. Several doctors worked on me in the emergency room, but their concern was that they could not get my blood pressure down. They told my wife that she might need to call the family to the hospital. I was so stressed that my body felt as if it were shutting down. My wife's mother and father came from Ft. Worth to keep the kids. Wanda was praying for me constantly and did not know what the outcome would be. This went on for three long days. The medicine did not help; my pressure was still high.

The third morning around two o'clock, I remembered a passage of Scripture that I was taught in church when I was a child. It was the twenty-third Psalm.

The Lord is my shepherd; I shall not want.
He makes me to lie down in green pastures;
He leads me beside the still waters.
He restores my soul;
He leads me in the paths of righteousness

for His name's sake.
Yea, though I walk through the
valley of the shadow of death,
I will fear no evil;
For You are with me;
Your rod and Your staff, they comfort me.
You prepare a table before me
In the presence of my enemies;
You anoint my head with oil;
My cup runs over.
Surely goodness and mercy shall follow me
All the days of my life;
And I will dwell in the house of the Lord
Forever.

I meditated on those verses for a couple of hours. I went verse by verse to see how it applied to my life. It was at that time that a peace from the Lord covered me completely. He impressed on my heart that I needed to do things differently. I needed to make some adjustments in my priorities. The Lord assured me that He had my back. The morning came, and about eight o'clock, my blood pressure had gone down to normal. The nurses and doctors were so surprised that they continued monitoring me for a couple of hours in ICU. They then released me to go home. I knew that things had to change concerning my work schedule.

My pastor visited me at the hospital and prayed for my family and was a dedicated pastor who loved and cared for his flock. One of the greatest lessons I learned from him was on a Wednesday night worship service. During the offering time, the Spirit moved him to ask if there were any single parents who did not have any money to place in the offering plate. Five single parents stood up, and he asked them to come forward. He went into his own pocket and gave each of them one hundred dollars. He shared that was for them. Then he gave each one of them five dollars to put in the offering plate. I will never forget the looks and the tears of these five people. It was as if they were on the brink of despair, but this gave them new inspiration. I have thought about that over the years and have strived to encourage others in that way.

I decided after my hospitalization that I needed to slow down and spend more time with God in the Word. I also needed to take better care of myself, exercise regularly, spend quality time with my family, and learn how to work smarter, not harder. It was after one of my morning quiet times with the Lord that I went to work. My pastor asked me how I was doing. I told him I was better. He said something to me that I shall never forget. I am still using that bit of advice twenty-five years later. He said he did not hire me to be a professional worker, but to be a professional thinker. He advised me to pray and think over my projects. Then I needed to train the right people to finish the project as I moved on to plan the next one. The wisdom was that I needed to see the vision, bathe it in prayer, delegate responsibility to fulfill the vision to the right people, and then train them how to complete the project. My job was to follow up by making sure everything was on course and then move to the next project. My wife and I had been Commission as Missionaries to the Home Mission Board in Memphis Tennessee. This prepared me for my following move to the corporate office of a National Missions Agency called the Home Mission Board. Its name was later changed to North American Mission Board. Its headquarters were in Atlanta, Georgia, and over four hundred people were employed there. I spent the next twelve years as a denominational worker.

Again the hand of the Lord intervened in my life. One of the singles from my church in Houston recommended me to his brother, for another job there in Atlanta. His brother was the director of Black Church Extension Program. He interviewed me for the job and offered me the position. I was one of three associates. Our responsibility was to travel and work in different states with associates to encourage African American ministers to start new churches. Part of our job was to put together a financial package and to help in the training of these perspective pastors. I travelled over one hundred days a year.

Chapter Seven:

PRIORITIES IN THE JOURNEY

E ven though I loved my work, I realized I had another priority that needed some adjustment. I was convicted that I needed to put my family second in my life instead of the church. I thank God for my wife who nurtured our kids while I was away. She had a major responsibility herself because she was the administrator of a church with five thousand members, but God blessed us because our three children have done well. We learned how to juggle our schedules so that we could make our children's major meetings. I coached my sons' baseball teams. I would look at my calendar and block out certain days to be involved in their lives. Since our daughter did not participate in sports, she spent her time reading.

My wife and I scheduled date nights to undergird our relationship and to keep the romance alive. We were both family oriented. My grandmother would stress to me as I was growing up how important being a good husband and treating my wife with respect were in a marriage. Wanda's parents, Mr. and Mrs. J.B. Lee, had been married for over fifty years. They were great examples for us to pattern our marriage after and to seek advice for staying married. They were people of integrity who provided economical help when we needed it. Mr. Lee, an extremely intelligent man, was a great strategist who could solve complicated issues. I enjoyed listening to his advice and absorbing his vast wisdom. He worked hard. Mrs. Lee, a wonderful encourager, was blessed with the gift of hospitality. Their home was always a refuge for family and friends to come by and share their troubles or their joys as they munched on goodies that Mrs. Lee had made.

In the later years of their life, we took them on trips. Mr. Lee had a sense of humor. I had a speaking engagement at one of the universities, and they went with us. I was driving back home after the engagement. Mr. Lee and I were talking. Since I am not good with directions, I took a wrong turn. Mr. Lee remarked he thought we were going the wrong way. I assured him that I was on the right road. Sure enough, I was headed back to the place where I had spoken. Well, it was dark, and I probably just got confused. I wish that were the case, but I have been known to get lost even in the daylight. We have laughed about that experience over the years.

My family life experiences spilled over to the lives of the church planting pastors and their families. I tried to instill in them this priority list: God, first; family, second; and church work, third. I found when I put God first in my life, He gave me a better perspective concerning the other two priorities.

Church planting is hard work and can be rough on family relationships because it takes so much time to get a church off the ground. A successful church planter has to make so many visits per week to get even a small percentage of people to come and be a part of the new church. Almost all church planters have to have a full time job in order to support their families since pastors receive salaries from the tithes and offerings of the congregation. It can be discouraging to make so many visits and only a handful of people show up for services. I felt part of my job was to keep the pastors from becoming discouraged over the slow progress in starting a new church. Many of the new pastors had no formal or seminary training for this particular ministry. I became their sounding board as they bounced ideas off me concerning the ministry. I shared the information that I had gained from my own experiences. Sadly, for every four churches started, only one church will make it. This statistic puts tremendous pressure on these new pastors. Some did not make it, and others were teetering on the brink of letting the church go.

I was in this position for about a year; then I was promoted to Director of Black Evangelism for the Convention. I traveled even more, trying to help the African American pastors to reach their communities with the gospel. I would conduct training sessions in outreach. The gospel, according to Mark 1:17, says, "And Jesus said unto them, 'Come ye after me, and I will make you to become fishers of men." I must admit that I don't know much about fishing, but not all fish eat the same bait. The message never changes. Jesus came down from heaven and was crucified on the cross for our sins. He stayed in the grave for three days and was resurrected on a Sunday morning with all power in His hands. This message will last until the end of time, but what does change is the methodology from one generation until the next. I tried to help pastors see the different needs in their own communities and make those their fishing points.

Dr. Darryl Robinson, the Vice President of Evangelism for the North American Mission Board, wrote a book titled *Total Church Life*. I took the skeleton of his book and put my own meat on it. I put together a five-hour evangelism training presentation. It has been effective in all different cultures because it is inspirational, informative, and educational. I thank God that I am still using that seminar, which is still relevant twenty years later.

The Home Mission Board became the North American Mission Board, and I was promoted to Multicultural Evangelism Manager. I had a staff comprised of two Korean associates and one Korean secretary. They taught me to take a closer look at each culture as I worked with different ethnic groups. I learned to listen closely and look deeper into the customs and values of each culture. These three workers met each morning before going to work to pray. They also pointed out that their culture held senior citizens in high esteem. When I attended a State Evangelism Conference, I was introduced to an older lady from the Pima Indian tribe who was asked to pray for the convention. She prayed with such conviction as she cried out to God for help in reaching the people from her tribe for Christ. The sincerity in her prayer brought tears to the eyes of many of those in attendance. Her prayer caused me to pray for the Pima Indians for fifteen years. My family always knew I closed my prayer, asking God to save the Pima Indians.

I had taken Spanish from the seventh grade through my sophomore year in college. I was able to use this knowledge as the Lord allowed me to preach a sermon in Spanish. The audience was quite surprised, as was I. Speaking Spanish built a trust level faster than normal because I had made the effort to learn and to communicate in their native language. My Spanish skills were helpful as I traveled and spent the night in various hotels. Many hotels employ Spanish-speaking employees. I would greet them with "Hola! Como estas?" That translates as, "Hello! How are you?" They would smile and reply, "Muy bien," which means, "Very well." I wish I had kept up with my Spanish skills because of the growing number of Hispanics living in the United States.

My youngest son married a wonderful young lady from El Salvador. Perhaps I could persuade her to help me brush up on my Spanish. Even though I am not fluent in Spanish, I can remember several words' meaning as I listen to their conversations. I know how to say hello in Chinese and Korean, and I know a few Russian phrases. As the multicultural manager, I have visited with Vietnamese, Japanese, German, and African people.

One of my greatest highlights was the time I was asked to attend the first Hispanic Prayer Breakfast in Washington, D.C. where President Bush was the speaker. I think he tried to figure out who I was and why I was there. This conference brought Hispanic leaders from all over the country. These leaders were well organized and could offer a lot to our society. I learned as I visited these different ethnic groups that all of us were on the brink of something important.

Chapter Eight:

HIGHER GROUND

I worked at a national mission agency called the North American Mission Board for twelve years. I loved my job, but I was beginning to get a little restless. That feeling had begun five years earlier at one of our African American Conferences. We named the conference, "Black Church Week." Pastors and lay people came together from all over the country for training in evangelism, Sunday school, church planting, music, and many other relevant workshops. Dr. Robert Smith, a preaching professor at Besson Seminary in Alabama, is one of the most profound preachers in the world, in my opinion. At the conference, he preached a message on Moses and how he got restless in the palace because his heart was leading him to the fields. That message haunted me for the next five years until an incident occurred that changed the direction of our family life.

The North American Mission Board was considered the palace by many Southern Baptist Churches because of the travel, training, and resources. I went there when I was thirty-seven years old. We had come to Atlanta when our son was in the first grade. He had always been a big, healthy kid. Even when he was born, he weighed nine pounds and eight ounces. Marcus was a great athlete, especially in baseball. He became close to two young men at school. He played on the baseball team with Bryan, and he just hung out with Randell. I called them "the three amigos."

One day at school, some of the kids were making fun of my son Marcus because of his weight. Even though Bryan, his friend, was small in stature, he told the older kid, "You can't make fun of my friend."

The other kid replied, "I will beat you up."

Bryan answered, "That might be the case, but Marcus is still my friend."

Marcus and Bryan became close friends as David and Jonathan, Saul's son, had done as recorded in the Old Testament. Marcus's positions were pitcher and first base, and Bryan played pitcher and shortstop. Bryan was a good hitter. I remember him hitting a home run off of Marcus. Marcus tipped his hat to him to acknowledge his great hit. When Marcus came to bat, Bryan was pitching. Marcus hit a home run, and Bryan in turn tipped his hat to Marcus. They were great competitors. Even though they played on different teams during the school year, they played together in the summer with a traveling team. Bryan's father, Craig Griffin, was their coach. Marcus stayed over at the Griffin house about as much as he stayed home. Bryan in turn stayed over at our house a lot. They both shared the dream of playing college baseball.

The Lord blessed us with a new house in 1999 that we had built. The main drawback was that we were located in a different school zone. Even though they did not attend the same school, they still remained close. An event happened their junior year that changed all our lives. One weekend Wanda, my wife, took Marcus to the doctor. He was diagnosed with an upper respiratory infection. He still wanted to spend the night at Bryan's so he could see him play basketball at his school. Normally, Wanda would have dropped him off at Bryan's, but that day she insisted he stay at home to take his medicine. We found out later that Bryan, one of the kindest young men I know, had taken several of his teammates home. It was raining that night. As he was headed home, he dropped something. When he looked up, another car was headed toward him. He must have overcorrected because his car hit a brick mailbox, and he was killed instantly.

I had just finished a revival in Maryland, and I was waiting to catch a flight home. Wanda called me crying and told me that I needed to come home quickly. When I quizzed her about her needing me, she recounted the sad story of Bryan's death. I was stunned with the news, and I felt as if my heart would break as I began to weep. He was like a son to our family. I mulled over all that Wanda had told me on the flight home. Once I arrived home, we went over to the Griffin's where we hugged and cried together with Julie, Craig, and the family. They asked me to do the eulogy, and I gladly accepted this honor. Even though it felt as if I were doing my own son's funeral, God gave me strength to get though the message.

A large crowd of students from Dunwoody High School attended the service. They were broken hearted. Many had attended the wake the night before. The wake, which began at 6:00 P.M. and ended at 9:00 P.M., was jammed-packed because the Griffins lived in a close community. The Griffins allowed Marcus to come early so that he could have private time to say good-bye to Bryan. I watched my son Marcus, who sat for over four hours on the front seat, never say a word. This incident changed him drastically. He withdrew into a shell and quit talking much to anyone. He was on the edge of depression. Our whole family was at a loss for words. I knew that I, as the spiritual head of the household, needed to do something. My mind drifted back to my grandmother and her teachings. I dropped to my knees in prayer. The Lord led me to do a forty-day fast, only drinking juice all day and eating one meal around 6:00 P.M. The Lord spoke to me in many ways as I prayed for my son and for the Griffins.

During that time of fasting, I was offered a prospective job in Philadelphia. I went to speak at a church in Northern Virginia for a pastor that I have known for over six years. At lunch I talked to him about the position in Philadelphia. He said that was a good place- ment, but he had a position that he needed to fill. He offered me the position of Director for Congregational Care and Evangelism. He had been trying to fill that position, but he had not found a compatible person for that particular post. Wanda and I began to pray for guidance. The Lord gave us the signal to take the position. They also offered Wanda a job on staff as an administrative assistant. This position did not require traveling, and I had more time at home to encourage my son. Marcus would complete his senior year in Virginia. It was not easy to make friends as a new student in the senior year of high school or to make the baseball team. I was able to make almost all of his baseball games. However, Marcus and our whole family still had a hole in our hearts over the death of Bryan.

Accepting that position finally stopped that sermon that I had heard five years earlier about Moses leaving the palace from nagging me because the church was considered the field that was ripe for harvest. I knew I had followed God's leading. My grandmother always taught me to lean on the Lord and His Word.

Isaiah 43:2 says: "When thou passeth through the waters, I will be with thee; and through the rivers, they shall not overflow thee; when thou walketh through the fire, thou shall not be burned; neither shall the flame kindle upon thee."

The Lord is great and mighty to be praised.

This church had many good people in it. The make-up was different from any other church that I had been a part of. It was about forty percent military. We had a general in our leadership team. He was sharp and blessed to have a great strategic mind. Several Colonels, who were leaders in their own right, were also members. People from the Pentagon, C.I.A., F.B.I., lawyers, doctors, engineers, teachers, executives of all types, and people who worked on the Hill attended our church. Most of the members were well educated, having, at the least, a master's degree.

The first two years, there was a learning curve for me. The church people were guarded because of the high-level positions they held. However, once they came through the church doors, they put their positions aside. They observed me closely to see if I was going to be there long. I made some headway, but I don't think I was completely successful my first two years there.

A pastor from another state called to ask if he could visit with my wife and me. He was on his way to Russia to see how their mission project was doing. He took us to a fancy restaurant, and as he talked, we listened with interest. His church was almost twice the size of the church at which I presently served. He wanted me to be on his executive staff in charge of missions and outreach. This included local and international missions. I would be flying all over the world to manage mission opportunities. He even offered my wife a job on his church staff. It sounded good. When he returned from Russia, he made provisions for Wanda and me to spend a weekend at his location so we could visit his church and observe its core leadership. I would also preach that Sunday. I had preached at that church several times in the past. We had a good time, but as always before we made a move, we prayed for the Lord's guidance. The Lord did not give us a peace about moving, and I felt that He impressed on me that our work at our present location was not finished. Wanda suggested I return to graduate school to prepare myself for this distinguished congregation. I looked at her with a strange look because I did not feel led to do that. I reminded her that I had gotten my master's degree over twenty-five years ago. She felt that I needed to update my education and retool for the new challenge. She is a wise woman, and I have learned over the years that she was always on point. My son was on campus at Liberty University, so my wife and I enrolled in their online program.

In graduate school I pursued a master's degree in marriage and family therapy. My wife majored in psychology. We both worked full-time jobs, came home to eat, and then went downstairs to work on our class assignments from 9:00 P.M. until 1:00 A.M. We would get up at 6:45 A.M. the next day to follow the same routine. We did this for three years. Online education was new to me because I had always studied on campus. I had to learn how to work the computer because all of my lessons, tests, papers, and group meetings were done online. I thank God for my wife who not only typed her papers, but mine also. Since I was not a good typist, her shouldering the added typing placed more stress on her, but she never complained. She always encouraged me because I had to adjust my way of thinking about education. It was tough going back to school when you are in your fifties and have been out of school for many years. I had completed thirty-three hours in my chosen field.

We had been at the church for five years. The members realized we would be there for a while, so they began to trust us. My counseling sessions took off, and I was busy day and night. We had created an environment of trust so they felt comfortable to come by for counseling. My average counseling sessions in the South were thirty minutes blocks of time, but for this church it was much longer than that. I asked my wife to meet with us when we met away from the church. The wives were happy to hear advice from a woman's perspective. Since we never violated that trust, our counseling sessions increased.

In June of 2010, my pastor and I went to the Southern Baptist Convention. He nominated me for a trustee on the International Mission Board. The committee approved me for that position. There were approximately ninety trustees, and I think I was the seventh African American to serve in that office in 150 years. My wife was so proud of me when I told her the news. We met every quarter at a predetermined location. Part of our responsibility was to make decisions on the missionaries who were looking to be confirmed. The missionary services on Wednesdays were always a highlight as we heard their testimonies and the receiving of their commission to different parts of the world. I felt special on those Wednesdays because they carried us to the church where the commissioning service was held in nice buses. This group of trustees oversaw nearly five thousand missionaries from all over the world. I had the privilege of serving a three-year term and was asked to serve a second term.

In May of 2013, my son had just graduated from Liberty University. We were so proud of him. One of his high school teachers had told him that he probably was not a good candidate for college so he needed to look at a trade school. His goal had always been to play baseball in college. We always taught him not to let other people discourage him from accomplishing his dream.

Graduation Day was extremely hot, but for some reason I was so cold that I used a blanket to cover myself. Wanda was concerned because I didn't look well at all. We made it through the ceremony on Saturday, and Monday morning I was scheduled to leave for the trustee meeting in Nashville, Tennessee. I didn't feel like going, but I had a responsibility to be there to encourage our missionaries. Wanda noticed that Sunday evening after church, my stomach looked big. I told her that I would work out and trim down once I got there.

I made it to the hotel in Nashville and called to pray for one of our member's mother who had cancer. The next morning, I was sitting in one of the committee meetings when I suddenly felt a sharp pain in my chest that I had never experienced before. Somehow I made it to my room and lay down, hoping the pain would soon pass. After an hour, I went down to see my secretary to tell her that I needed to go to the hospital. I lay on the floor and passed out. I knew I was ill because I would never have lain on the floor in my suit.

The next thing I remember was the ambulance coming to take me to the hospital. One of our trustees was a doctor, and he rode to the hospital with me. They ran tests and first felt the problem was my spleen. When the surgeon opened me up, he found that the problem was greater than the spleen. They packed me with as much gauze as they could and told me that I needed to be transferred to another hospital. The doctor who had come with me called my wife while I was in surgery and told her that she needed to come as soon as possible. He thought that I had had a heart attack. Wanda rushed to Nashville, and the doctor informed her that I had cancer in my stomach, esophagus, and spleen. I was not aware of the diagnosis since I was slipping in and out of a coma.

After I arrived at the other hospital, they rushed me to surgery. After several hours, the doctor came out and told Wanda that he had removed part of my stomach, part of my esophagus, and my spleen. He told her that he had gotten all the cancer, but the real problem was putting me back together again. God gave me Dr. Polk, one of best cancer doctors in the United States, who was well known throughout the world. He was a specialist in stomach cancer. He turned me over to Dr. Roberts, one of the best surgeons in the country. His job was to try to pull everything together that had been cut out of me during surgery. There was one hole in my stomach that they did not close up. My wife asked the doctor if my heart could handle another surgery. He reassured her that my heart was one of the strongest things in my body. They operated on me several times. The final surgery was to close that opening. I was sent for tests prior to the surgery to pinpoint the location of the hole. As they looked for it, they found it had miraculously disappeared.

My wife called the kids to get to Nashville because it didn't look good for me. My daughter, who lived in Texas, was the first to arrive. She stayed about a week with my wife. It was touch and go for me, and the doctors were not sure if I would recover. I overheard my daughter talking to her mother. She was asking her if I knew I had cancer. I was in I.C.U. for over about three weeks. It had to be hard on my wife to see me connected to all those machines. I had a team of seven doctors that would meet daily to discuss the best method of treatment for me. My son and his wife also came to see me.

Wanda stayed with me for over six weeks. I don't believe I could have recovered if she had not been there the whole time. She monitored my condition every day by quizzing the doctors about my status. They told her I was very ill, and all we could do was wait to see how I responded to treatment. She spent most of the day alone, praying and wondering if I was going to pull through. A couple from our church came down to spend time with Wanda and to check on my progress.

Wanda had just begun a new job with the county two days before she got the call that I was ill. When she arrived at the hospital and saw the condition that I was in, she called her boss to tell him she needed to resign her job. They kept her on the pay roll for another two weeks to see if she would be able to come back to work.

Since she was such a good administrator, they didn't want to lose her. Seeing that my illness was going to be lengthy, she called her boss back two weeks later to officially resign. Day after day, she prayed to God.

After my second surgery, I was extremely tired. I told her that I loved her, but I wasn't going to make it. I felt that I was on the brink of death and was prepared to be with the Lord. She shared with me that she had returned to the hotel to cry and pray for hours. She asked the Lord to not take her husband and to heal him from this dreaded disease. Even though the process was slow, my health began to improve. There were ups and downs every day. My lungs collapsed, and the doctors felt I was headed toward renal failure.

I thank God for the nurses who were so helpful and encouraging. One African American nurse in I.C.U. kept encouraging me to get better so I could move to a less critical floor. One day, she combed my hair and put some grease on it. She wanted to shave me, but I told her I didn't know if my wife would approve of her touching my face. When my wife returned to the hospital, she was surprised how I looked, but remarked that I needed a shave. The nurse told her that she wanted to shave me, but I wasn't sure how Wanda would feel about that. Wanda told her there was no problem with her shaving me. My time in I.C.U. had almost expired, so the doctors wanted to move me to another floor. They assured Wanda that if my condition worsened that they would return me to I.C.U.

One of the nurses later shared that when I was transferred to the new floor, she had thought to herself that I would not make it. I had been in the new room a few days when I got a staph infection. The doctors worked with me diligently because this alone could have killed me. I finally got over the infection after many days. Wanda stayed by my side the whole time. Four people came down to see me. More church members wanted to come, but leadership shared that I was gravely ill and their prayers would be more helpful.

The first day that I went to the hospital, one of our prominent members spoke to my wife and said their family was going to overnight us some money to relieve the pressure on my wife and the cost of our extended stay. We still are good friends with this wonderful family. The pastor came down to see us. Many of the church members sent cards with money in them. They were a loving group of people who prayed for us and blessed us monetarily. The nurses who cared for me were all good, but one nurse stands out in my memory. This nurse Vivian found out that I was a preacher. She was a believer and told me that I had to get up because I was needed to share the gospel with other people. I had not walked in over a month. Vivian told Wanda that she intended to get me out of the bed and help me to start walking. Several days later Wanda rounded the corner of the hall and saw me walking with the aid of a walker. I will never forget the kindness of Vivian.

The only thing that I was allowed to put in my mouth was water that dripped off a sponge. I was fed through an IV. A week later, the doctors added popsicles to my diet. Vivian asked me for my favorite flavors. I later told her that I felt sorry for the nurses because they spent that night bringing to my room twenty-three halves of popsicles that I consumed. I must have been hungry. I think there needs to be a special day set aside to appreciate nurses.

Finally, I was able to leave the hospital, but we had to stay in a hotel for two weeks before my last appointment. I can never thank our church enough for putting my wife in a nice hotel, paying for car rental, and paying for her meals the entire time we were there. My mother, sister, her husband, and my niece came to see us when we moved to the hotel. We were so glad that they made the trip to visit us. My mother was about eighty-two years old, but she was in good health.

My wife was my nurse at the hotel. She made sure that my feeding machine was working. During the night when my food ran out, she got up and changed it. The doctor had given us a two months' supply of milk for the feeding tube. On the last visit to my doctor before we returned home, the feeding tube fell out of my stomach. He had surgically replace the tube once before. He looked puzzled about the feeding tube and then decided that I might not even need it any more. We explained to the doctor that for two weeks we had been eating at Piccadilly Cafeteria. I only ate soft foods such as potatoes covered in gravy. My stomach was not strong enough to tolerate meat. I went home without the feeding tube. God is so good.

The International Mission Board flew us home first class. Many of them came by to pray for us. They had sent emails all over the country and to our missionaries abroad to pray for my recovery. Heads of agencies and the president of the International Mission Board came by to visit with us. We later learned churches from around the nation whose members were from varied cultures prayed for us, too.

I was still extremely weak when I returned home. I had difficulty walking. Wanda cared for and nursed me daily. Her mother came to stay with us for three months and did all the cooking. I was still sick because I was taking a chemo pill. I was on that medication for three years. The chemo had wiped me out. I was 255 pounds when I went into the hospital. I weighed 168 pounds when I returned home. The first year at home, I spent most of my time in bed. I would get up daily to walk short distances. Almost a year passed, and I was not able to go to work, but they paid me my full salary. We ended up going back home to Ft. Worth, Texas. We asked the pastor if the church could pay for our move. The leadership agreed to pay the costly charge. My cousin, Reverend Lou Phillips, gave us a going away party, where special friends came to say goodbye and to give us cards with money inside. The goodbye was tearful and sad.

The first year at home I was weak and not able to do very much because of the chemo. Wanda took me to the numerous doctors' appointments and tried to get me out of the house. I had been in depression for three years. I felt safe at home. Halfway through the year, I got involved with a cancer support group in Keller, Texas, at the Methodist Hospital. Our director Cindy was encouraging. We met frequently, and I began to listen to the stories of other people who had stage four cancer. They were so upbeat and lived each day to the fullest. We shared our testimonies and became a family. I looked forward every week to our meetings. Each month we had a schedule full of activities such as movie night, sewing, and yoga. A specialist came to share different aspects of cancer and how to cope with this disease. We brought our spouses to the dinners that we had where we realized we were not alone in this battle. It was comforting to know other people had gone through what we were experiencing and had survived.

The second year, my wife went to Baylor Medical Center in Grapevine, Texas, for surgery. I went with her. The lady chaplain came to pray for her that morning as she was waiting to be taken to the operating room. When the chaplain left, I realized that I could handle being a chaplain in the hospital in my present condition. Wanda encouraged me to put my paperwork in to apply as a volunteer chaplain there. I was approved and have been volunteering for over a year and three months.

At the same time, the Lord spoke to my heart that I needed to begin working out to get my strength back. When I left the hospital in Nashville, I could not lift even a pencil. A year and three months later, my schedule changed drastically. I joined a fitness facility and worked out for two hours, four times a week. I only worked with twenty-pound weights, but I did a lot of repetitions. It strengthened my core, and now I feel better than I have felt in thirty years. Our oldest son Marlin came to town, and I asked him to go workout with me. He joined me, but after thirty minutes, he asked if I were ready to leave. I told him that I still had an hour and a half left to work. When we returned, he told his mother that he could not believe that I had enough stamina to work out that long. He asked her if I intended to try out for the Dallas Cowboys. I give God all the glory. He alone is worthy to be praised.

I have shared my testimony with hundreds of people at the hospital. I have spoken with doctors, nurses, patients, family members, and even some of their neighbors. Those words of survival have brought joy and hope to so many people. It is amazing that the thing that almost killed me has brought a new lease on life to others. I have had many experiences of sharing in the hospital, but two stick out in my memory. I went to visit a patient, but before I knocked on the door, a nurse approached me and told me that the lady and her daughter were such a blessing. She was an African American lady who was a prophetess. I listened to her for a while and then shared my testimony. I stayed in the room for about an hour talking to her and her daughter. Right before I got up to leave, she said to me she wanted to tell me something. She saw two things that were going to happen in my life: harvest and jubilee. Since that time, I have been experiencing both of them in the form of miracles.

The second person that stood out in my visits was brought to me by a nurse. She explained this man and wife had just received bad news. She told me that the doctor had just given him the diagnosis of cancer. Knowing my story, the nurse felt that I could possibly bring comfort to them. I went in to talk with both of them and listened to them with compassion. I shared my testimony with him, and it brought joy to his face. He made a statement that startled me. He said he had been waiting all day for me. I am sure that I had a puzzled look on my face. He pointed out that I was like Johnny Appleseed. I shared the Word of God through dropping the seeds of my life and that God would supply all my needs in order to do that ministry.

I left the hospital that day contemplating what he had just told me. God truly had provided for my family, and the doors of ministry had begun to open back up again. God gave me a Scripture that I meditated on for the next three years. John 9:4 states, "I must work the works of Him that sent me while it is day; the night cometh when no man can work." I received this verse at the Texas African American Conference. God spoke to my heart that it had been night, but a new day was coming for me. He has given me a second wind to start the next chapter of ministry. I thought that ministry was over, but God had just given me rest for four years. Now it was time to go back and serve Him again.

Chapter Nine:

LIVING ON THE BRINK

One Saturday evening, I pondered over my life, which had many different twists and turns. It had been a little over three years since my cancer had gone into remission. I had started to preach which was a miracle because my doctors had shared with me that there was a possibility that I would never preach again because of all my surgeries. I had a paralyzed right diaphragm, which caused some breathing issues. I had two words to say about that statement, and those words were: "BUT GOD."

I had not preached in three years when I received an invitation to preach at Shiloh Missionary Baptist Church, whose pastor, for over fifty years, was the late Pastor A.E. Chew. On that day, my daughter, her husband, my grandbaby, my son, his wife, and my wonderful encouraging wife all attended the service. Three of my friends whom I had played basketball with forty years prior came, too. The Lord anointed me with His power to preach with authority that Sunday. I felt as if life was beginning again. I was back doing what I believed God had called me to do and what I loved doing. For three years, that joy had been taken away from me. The doors of opportunity for ministry had opened again. Not only was I allowed to preach, but I also was asked to lead seminars on evangelism. My world was back.

In August 2016, I was asked to go to Georgia to preach two services at a church that was celebrating its 102nd church anniversary.

This was the first preaching engagement out of state since my surgeries. My wife gladly accompanied me on this trip because she had been the administrator of this church from 1991 through 2000. The pastor of this mega church of over seven thousand members and I had been friends for over fifteen years. They had just built their new worship center. During this service, the pastor surprised my wife by asking her to stand so that he could present her with the Eagle award. This award was one of the highest awards bestowed on people for their excellent work and dedication. The church gave her a standing ovation. This not only blessed her heart, but it also showed her that her work had not been in vain. Of course, I was so proud of her. The pastor later shared with us in private that he had to hire three people to do the work that Wanda had done alone. Wanda is one of the most gifted administrators in the country, and her organizational skills are impeccable.

This was a good weekend. The highlight of that trip was meeting and taking a picture with the man who plays the President of the United States in the movie, Scandal. We headed home, tired and happy.

Our next out-of-state trip was to Northern Virginia in September. I was the guest speaker at this church that I had watched grow into a mega church over the past fifteen years. Earlier in my ministry, I had been given a vision to train and mentor five pastors whose churches had five hundred members. I watched them grow into mega churches. This church was one of them. I preached two services for their 150th church anniversary. It was a great time of renewal and refreshment for our spirits. Some of the key members of the church where Wanda and I had served on staff for years surprised us by coming to this service. My brother Leonard, my cousin Beverly, and my cousin, Lou Phillips, and his wife came to the celebration. We returned home that Sunday night, happy with the support of our friends there in Virginia.

On Monday morning I started throwing up blood, and Wanda took me to the hospital. I was at Grapevine Baylor and Scott & White Hospital for three days. The doctors transferred me to Baylor and Scott & White Hospital in Dallas. After thirteen days and many tests, the diagnosis was that my cancer had returned with a vengeance. I began to wonder why the Lord had allowed this to happen and why He had chosen this time. My mind drifted back to almost five years prior. Again, my wife was right there by my side. She took without pay family medical leave from her job. She helped to nurse me back to life again. The doctors placed me on chemo, which I dreaded.

After being out of the hospital for three weeks, Wanda and I made a follow up visit with my primary doctor. She was glad to see us. I handed her a thick report, which lay people could not read or understand, concerning my treatment that the doctors had used while I was in the hospital. As she was reading the report, she kept saying, "Somebody save him!" She turned, page after page, repeating the same phrase. I had lost a lot of blood and had received several transfusions. I did not know until then that I was on the brink of death, again. Our doctor took her time going over the report with us and did not try to rush us out of the office. As we left, she took our hands and prayed for us. I am so blessed to have a Christian doctor who loves the Lord.

Wanda and I had no idea how we would make it financially since she had taken off three months without pay. God always provides for His children. The next six months were rough for me, and I wondered if I was going to make it. The process was slow, and the chemo made me tired and weak. I had a lot of time to think, pray, and allow the Lord to speak to me afresh and anew. As the Lord strengthened my body, He also built up my faith.

At the end of those six months, the Lord spoke to my heart instructing me that it was time to return to my work in chaplaincy. When I visited the chaplain in the hospital, he looked as if he had seen a ghost. He had seen me in the beginning in the hospital and had noticed that I was in dire condition. He expressed his pleasure in seeing me, but he quizzed me to see if I was ready to return to work. I assured him that I was ready to begin sharing Christ with those who were troubled. After he agreed that I was ready, I told him I would work only Monday afternoons in the beginning.

When I went to get my volunteer time card reset, I ran into Maurine Hair, the head of all volunteers at Grapevine Baylor Scott & White Hospital. She was so excited to see me that she gave me a big embrace. Perhaps she had felt that she would never see me again volunteering. I returned to my duties with more life than ever, encouraging patients, spouses, doctors, nurses, neighbors, relatives, and care providers. I knew God had placed me there to continue my ministry. I also started going back to my cancer support group on Thursdays, and the other clients were elated to see me.

One Thursday afternoon Cindy, the director of this Cancer Support Center in Tarrant County, asked me if I would teach a seminar on cancer and spirituality. I was surprised, but I agreed. I had about a month to prepare. I was thrilled about the opportunity because those cancer support centers are not religion-based. We had a good crowd that night, and I shared my testimony and the importance of knowing Jesus Christ as their personal Lord and Savior. Several people stayed and talked to me for a long time. I had called my doctor two hours before the meeting to ask her to pray for me. I had told her where the meeting would be held. The seminar was from 6:30 P.M. to 8:00 P.M. To my great surprise, she showed up to support me. I was so grateful because I know doctors have busy schedules aside from having their own families. She came with little notice, and that act blessed my heart greatly. I introduced her as my doctor to the group, and they were blown away. Cindy told me later that she had taken a survey concerning the seminar, and the results were so good that she wanted to ask her boss to let me lead this seminar once a month. She cautioned me not to get my hopes up because this was not the way these groups had been conducted before. Three weeks later, she announced to the group that I would be leading this seminar every month. She and her staff were not allowed to be involved, but I would have the building to share with cancer survivors and their families. I have also started working out two or three days a week. Our God is so good!

Chapter Ten

One Sunday after church eight years ago, a young woman with tears in her eyes approached me and said she needed to talk to me. My daughter was home from out of town, and I wanted to spend as much time with her as possible. My wife looked at me and told me to go talk with her. She said they would wait while I did. This young lady shared that she had a word for me from the Lord. I listened intently to her. She recounted God had told her to tell me not to worry about my house or car. In fact, God would provide a luxury car for me. I looked at her strangely because my present car was breaking down. We had tried to trade it in, but the dealership didn't want my old car. Fairfax County is one of the richest counties in the United States. The housing market is always off the charts. She informed me that someone was going to give me some money and I was to spend some of it on myself. I was intrigued because I had never seen her before at our church, even though she was a member. After she shared with me, I pondered over those things in my heart. I told my wife and daughter what she had said, and they looked stunned. The following Wednesday, we got a call from the church that one of the young ladies had died in her sleep. To my surprise, it was the lady who had shared her message from God with me. I told my wife, and that broke Wanda's heart.

The young lady's family came in from out of state to make the funeral arrangements. We were sitting around the conference table talking about the young lady with her sisters. They were expressing their pain at the loss, but one of the sisters said something that grabbed my attention. She explained that her sister was known as a prophetess. Every word that the young lady had given me has come true, even though she did not live to see it happen.

The Lord allowed us to get a home located behind the gates of an exclusive country club. We went to the Chevy car lot looking for a car, but I remembered what she had said. We drove into a car lot that we would never have considered because of the expensive vehicles. We left that night driving a brand new Land Rover. Two years later, God blessed us with a big check. We had never seen a check this big before. To put all of this in context, we struggled to do God's will. Both my wife and I were under a doctor's care, and our health was not good. We had always been taught to be faithful to the Lord, and He would meet our needs. The Word of God is true. Philippians 4:19 says, "But God shall supply all your need according to His riches in glory by Christ Jesus'"

One last note is that my oncologist ran a scan on my body several months after my cancer returned, and this scan showed all five tumors had shrunk by sixty percent. This Scripture ministered to my heart during this time.

Mark 4:35-40:

> *On the same day, when evening had come, He said to them, "Let us cross over to the other side." Now when they had left the multitude, they took Him along in the boat as He was. And other little boats were also with Him. And a great windstorm arose, and the waves beat into the boat, so that it was already filling. But He was in the stern, asleep on a pillow. And they awoke Him and said to Him, "Teacher, do you not care that we are perishing?" Then He arose and rebuked the wind, and said to the sea, "Peace, be still!" And the wind ceased and there was a great calm. But He said to them, "Why are you so fearful? How is it that you have no faith?"*

The disciples thought they were going to die on this journey. They forgot one thing. Christ was the one who told them to cross over to the other side. They realized all they needed was a word from the Lord to change their situation. So, it is with us. Just one word from the Lord changes everything.

ACKNOWLEDGMENTS

This book was not my original idea. My wife and I went by the rehab center where her cousin's mother was staying. She was not doing well, so we stopped by to pray with her. Christine Curl, one of her daughters, and I began to share about how God had worked in our lives. She suggested that I needed to write a book. I took on the challenge, and with the help of God, I completed most of it in eight days. God often uses wise counsel to plant His seeds in our mind. God impressed on my heart that I needed to go on a forty-day prayer vigil as I worked on this book. During that time, I was not to go to the hospital for visitation or to work out until those forty days were over. Every time that I have had problems and was on the edge of despair, He has always brought me through. I pray that this book speaks to the hearts and minds of those who are going through difficult times. Our God is faithful. He never promised we wouldn't have problems, but He promised He will walk with us through every one as He holds us up to accomplish the task He set for us.

I want to thank and acknowledge my wife Wanda who has supported me though out our marriage in the ups and downs. We have been married nearly forty years, and the Lord brought her into my life at a time when I was broken. She is an elegant lady with keen insight and wisdom beyond her years. She has a deep understanding of life and has such insight that she can predict the outcome of a situation before it happens. Her discernment has helped me look at life through different lenses. Not only is she a woman of many talents, but she is also a fantastic wife, mother, daughter, and friend. She is the love of my life and my best friend.

Another person I would like to acknowledge is my grandmother. Even though she is deceased, her spirit lives on in me, my children, and the people I meet. She prepared me for life by her lifestyle and the principles of God that she embedded in me. She loved me unconditionally and always took time to hear me and value me as a person. She did not have a great deal of education, but prayer was the center of her life. She made the best out of what she had and never complained. Grandmother, a modest woman, had a simple lifestyle with a deep daily walk with the Lord. She saw and nurtured in me what I could not see in myself. She prepared me to go across the United States telling people about Jesus Christ and meeting their needs as I could. She prepared me to be a man of God.

My mother is a faithful woman of God. I watched her lifestyle and her love for the Lord. She is a quiet lady who walked the Christian walk. I inherited my intellectual abilities from my mom, who is a smart lady.

I thank God for my editor, Elaine Seagler. She taught English for over forty years, which prepared her to edit this book. She edited this book while walking in deep waters as she cared for her ill husband. I was introduced to her by her daughter, Angela Niestemski, who is a chaplain at Grapevine Baylor Scott & White Hospital.

Special Thanks: Dr. Robert Smith who has been a mentor and family friend over the years. It was such a blessing for him to write the forward for my book.

CPSIA information can be obtained
at www.ICGtesting.com
Printed in the USA
BVOW09s1213220118

505965BV00015B/844/P

9 781545 617090